Bartholomew Gosnold

of

Otley and America

by

John Haden and Y7 Students of Woodbridge School, Suffolk

First published by Barny Books,
All rights reserved
Copyright © John Haden 2007

No part of this publication may be reproduced or transmitted in any way or by any means, including electronic storage and retrieval, without prior permission of the publisher.

ISBN No: 978-1-903172-90-2

Publishers: Barny Books
Hough on the Hill,
Grantham,
Lincolnshire
NG32 2BB

Tel: 01400 250246

Copies of this book and the others in the ARIES series may be obtained from:

Julian Bower Associates,
Julian Bower House, Louth,
Lincolnshire LN11 9QN. UK
Tel: 01507 601254

Please enclose cheque payable to 'Julian Bower Associates' with your order and add £1.00 per copy to cover postage and packing.   See   www.captainjohnsmith.co.uk   further details, and www.barnybooks.biz/ for publisher's details.

Contents

1. Waiting for the tide — 4
2. Suffolk roots — 8
3. Cambridge and the Law — 14
4. Seeking Norumbega — 29
5. Planning the great voyage — 43
6. Jamestown bound — 54
7. Jamestown survives – just — 65
8. Bones in the dirt — 68
9. Living at the Hall — 74

Postscript, Chronology, Sources and Thanks — 77

1. Waiting for the Tide

Captain Bartholomew Gosnold paced across the deck of his ship, four strides one way and four back, as the *Godspeed* lay at anchor in Blackwall Reach. Under her the black waters of the River Thames oozed upstream on the last of the rising tide. He had already checked her cables. She was well clear of the other ships moored nearer to Blackwall Steps. Earlier that month of December 1616, the *Susan Constant*, with Captain Newport in command, had swung into the path of another vessel coming up the congested waterway, and damage had been done. Gosnold could not afford such carelessness. Tomorrow, they sailed on the falling tide. Turning towards the lights of the City of London, Gosnold felt the soft westerly breeze. They would have a prosperous wind in the morning as they slipped their moorings and headed for the open sea.

Gosnold's ship, the *Godspeed*, by Georgia R.

For five years, he had been planning this voyage, ever since he had been forced to sail back to England from the shores of Cape Cod in the northern part of the land the English called Virginia. They had reached the Cape and landed on a nearby island planning to stay there over the winter to establish the first successful colony of Englishmen on the North American shore. But the extreme cold and their dwindling food supplies had undermined their resolve. They sailed back to England and the jeers of those who had stayed at home.

This time, they would succeed, of that he was sure. They had three ships, the *Susan Constant*, his own *Godspeed* and Captain Ratcliffe's little *Discovery*, now moored close by. Earlier that day, the Treasurer of the Virginia Company had sent a barge down-river to take them to Deptford, where Frances Drake's ship, the *Golden Hind*, was moored. Drake had sailed her right round the world and it had become the custom for the Captains of ships on any great voyage to dine on Drake's ship before weighing anchor.

London, the Thames and Blackwall, just north of the Isle of Dogs, from John Speed's 1611 map of London.

Gosnold sat down to dine with the leading men of the Virginia Company, and to drink a toast to the success of their great venture. Their planning had been better this time. The Company had raised money by selling shares in their joint-stock venture. The King himself had signed the Royal Warrant of their company authorising the voyage. A hand-picked company of one hundred and five men and boys had been recruited, mainly from London and the eastern Counties of England and tons of supplies had been packed into the holds of their three ships. Surely, this time they could not fail.

They knew the risks they faced. All the Captains and many of the crews of the three ships had sailed across the Atlantic to the Caribbean in search of rich pickings from the Spanish treasure ships in Queen Elizabeth's time. But even now when King James had made peace with Spain and stopped the English privateers from raiding the Spanish, it was not going to be easy to cross the ocean in such tiny ships. Many sailed from England and many never returned.

Captain Gosnold pulled his heavy seaman's cloak up around his shoulders against the cold December night and continued his pacing. He was sure he could trust his thirteen crewmen, drinking together in their cramped cabin in the stern of the ship. They were all experienced seamen, and most had sailed with him before. But what of the thirty nine men and boys now settled into what space they could find on gun-deck of the ship, and the other passengers sailing on the other ships? How would they fare on the long voyage out and in a strange land? Two were members of his own family. His younger brother Anthony and his second cousin, also Anthony, were young men who trusted Bartholomew to take them safely to Virginia.

Only one other family had three members risking their lives in this venture. George, William and Thomas Cassen were all labourers from London hoping to make their fortune in the New World. For them, life was already brutal and short. They had little to lose. Like the two other labourers on board, George Golding and William Unger, both from Suffolk, they had signed on for seven years to work for the Company before they could start working for themselves on land granted to them.

Another Suffolk man, Anas Todhill, travelled as the servant of Captain John Martin, and his son, also John. The father was a useful man to have on board as an experienced sea-captain who had sailed with Drake and had good links with the City of London. Thomas Cooper, also came from Suffolk. As a barber he had a useful skill to offer on a long voyage. Amongst the gentlemen, three came from Suffolk, William Brewster, Thomas Webb and George Golding. Finally there were two other experienced sea-captains who came from the area around Ipswich which Gosnold knew so well. The Captain of the *Discovery*, John Ratcliffe was also called Sicklemore, a south Suffolk name. The home of Captain Gabriel Archer lay across the River Orwell, in the County of Essex. He was without a command on this voyage, but well known to Gosnold as he had sailed with him on his earlier voyage to the northern coast of Virginia. Captain Newport himself had been born in the port of Harwich, where the Orwell estuary opens into the North Sea.

With one last check on her mooring ropes, Captain Bartholomew Gosnold turned into the aft cabin he shared with Garbniel Archer. By the dim light of a candle, he began to write a letter to his Uncle at Otley Hall.

2. Suffolk Roots

Suffolk in the early 17th Century

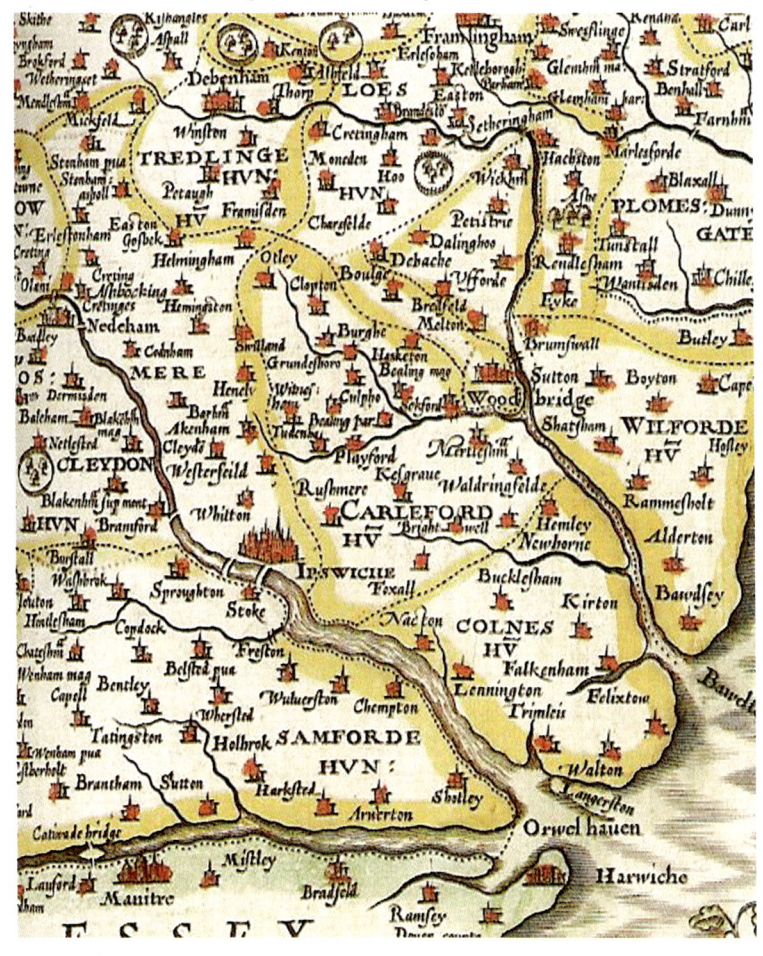

South Suffolk in John Speed's early seventeenth century map, showing the port of 'Harwiche' on the south bank of the 'Orwel Haven', the Town of 'Ipswiche' to the north-west on the river, the village of 'Otley' due north from 'Ipswiche' and the town of 'Woodbridge' to the north west of 'Ipswiche', on the River Deben.

Suffolk villages and churches

Timber framed houses in the village of Lavenham, Suffolk

Long Melford, one of the glorious 'wool' churches of Suffolk

  Suffolk, the county in which Bartholomew Gosnold was born, has many pretty villages of half-timbered cottages with brightly coloured and decorated plaster-work. Some like Lavenham are world famous, a community of weavers frozen in time when their rich trade in broad cloth was overtaken by new fabrics brought in from Europe. They left a village of pretty houses where few could afford to build new ones since the middle of the sixteenth century. Suffolk also has hundreds of fine medieval churches built of flint and stone as the area grew rich on the backs of sheep and English wool found a good market in the north of Europe.

The region is still called East Anglia, the land where the South Folk and the North Folk of the East Angles settled. In the centuries after the Romans left England, these Anglo-Saxon tribes swept in from lands across the North Sea. In Suffolk, they buried their king, Raedwald, in his long-ship at Sutton Hoo, near Woodbridge to be rediscovered with his jewelry and helmet 1400 years later. Their small farming communities grew into scattered villages linked by little more than bridle paths. Even today, Suffolk is a county of small villages with narrow winding roads and few major towns. Only Ipswich and Bury St Edmunds are of any size, and most of the County is still deeply rural. About six miles north of Ipswich, the settlement of Ota's Lea (or Meadow) became the village of Otley.

'It is not a big village, just a few houses with a post office that is the village shop. There is a pub and a church but you could drive through Otley and miss the church. The main feature of the village is Otley Hall, a very big old building, built mostly of brick and timber. Inside it is a big hall with brick open fireplaces. It has four bedrooms and a dining room, living room and a big garden with a nice pond.'

Otley is a working village as modest as Charlie C.'s description. The parish church of St Mary with its square tower of flint flushwork is hidden behind a high hedge.

The Parish Church of St.Mary, Otley by Sam D.

Otley Church Chancel by Micha K and the medieval font with carvings damaged during the Reformation.

But Otley is well worth visiting. Tucked away to the east of the main road is one of the finest Tudor hall-houses in all England, Otley Hall. Not far away to the south again, another fine Tudor mansion, Otley High House, has also miraculously survived about five hundred years. Both houses have strong links with the Gosnold family.

Otley Hall today

The family first lived in the Otley area when John Gosnold became tenant of the manor of Netherhall at the beginning of the fifteenth century. He is said to have built a house on the site, which was known as Netherhall Manor, but the Gosnolds did not buy the right to be Lords of the

Manor until much later. Between about 1512 and 1588, successive generations of the family built what is now Otley Hall, with its high chimneys, half-timbered wings and surrounding moat, the classic Elizabethan house. But was Bartholomew Gosnold born here?

Tracking down those born into Tudor England was made much easier by King Henry VIII. In about 1538, he decreed that a register had to be kept of all the children who were baptised in each English parish church, and all the marriages and burials at which the Vicar officiated. The register had to show names and dates and the family relationships. Most of these records have survived to this day and it is possible to discover where and when these events took place.

Unfortunately, the first registers for the parish church in Otley have not survived, so there is no formal record of when and where Bartholomew Gosnold was baptised, we can only work it out from later details of his life and the records of other members of his family.

The Family of Bartholomew Gosnold

Robert Gosnold 1st was Bartholomew Gosnold's great-grandfather. He came to Otley in 1512 and built Otley Hall which is where Bartholomew is said to have grown up. His son, Robert Gosnold 2nd had a son, also called Robert. He was Bartholomew's uncle and is known as Robert Gosnold 3rd. He lived in the hall with his own Gosnold children around the time that Queen Elizabeth 1st was on the throne. His brother was called Anthony and he was Bartholomew's father. Anthony had two sons so Bartholomew had a brother also called Anthony. *(by Jono L.)*

Robert Gosnold III's brother Anthony graduated from Cambridge University and trained as a lawyer at Gray's Inn in London. In 1570, he married a member of the Bacon family, Dorothy. Together they had nine children, two boys and seven girls. His sons were Bartholomew and Anthony. The name Bartholomew became fashionable in Protestant England after the massacre of French Protestants ordered by the Catholic King of France in August 1572, so it is likely that Bartholomew Gosnold was born in that year, although some think he was born in 1571.

His father lived in several places, Clopton, Grundisburgh and Otley, and just where Bartholomew was born is not known. It was 'somewhere near Ipswich'! Anthony Gosnold owned Otley High House from the time of his grandfather's death in 1572, and that could have been his son's birthplace. As here is no baptism record in any of the local churches, we simply do not know. Neither do we know where he went to school or whether like many boys of the time, he was educated at home by a tutor. The tradition at Otley Hall is that he joined the children of his uncle and was educated at the Hall with his cousins.

4. Cambridge and the Law

If Bartholomew did attend a local grammar school in the late 1570s and early 1580s, it could have been the school in Ipswich which Cardinal Wolsey started and which developed into Ipswich School. But as there are no records of pupils from this period, again, we simply do not know. What we do know is that Bartholomew Gosnold followed in the footsteps of his father and uncle to Cambridge University. He was admitted to Jesus College in 1587 as a 'sizer', one who paid for his lodgings, and completed his studies there in 1590.

The gatehouse to Jesus College, Cambridge, by Jenny A.

Learning at Cambridge

The students who went to Cambridge studied first what would now be termed a 'foundation course' in arts, grammar, logic and rhetoric – followed later by arithmetic, music, geometry and astronomy, leading to the degrees of bachelor and master. The teaching was conducted by masters who had themselves passed through the course and who had been approved or licensed by the whole body of their colleagues (the universitas or university) The teaching took the form of reading and explaining texts. The examinations were spoken rather than written, in which candidates were asked a series of questions. They had to defend their answers with opponents a little senior to themselves, and finally with the masters who had taught them. Some of the masters went on to advanced studies in divinity, law, and more rarely, medicine. (by Micha K.)

Middle Temple, the finest of the Elizabethan Inns of Court in London

When he had completed his degree at Jesus College, Cambridge, Bartholomew Gosnold followed his father and his Uncle to train as a lawyer. He first entered New Inn on his way to joining the Middle Temple, which with the Inner Temple, Gray's Inn and Lincoln's Inn made up the four Inns of Court. These were the professional bodies which had the exclusive right to train and admit lawyers to the role of barrister in the courts of England, a right which they have enjoyed since the 14th Century and still enjoy. To be 'called to the bar' is to be admitted as a fully qualified barrister having served as a member of an Inn of Court, a process which involved much legal training, but also attending dinners and networking with lawyers.

The Inns were a combination of exclusive dining club and a place to work. Barristers in their 'chambers' could be 'briefed' to defend or prosecute cases which came before the criminal and civil courts. Strategically sited between the London's commercial centre in the City to the east, and the government in what is still called the Palace of Westminster to the west, the lawyers of the Inns of Court made a good living out of commerce and government. They still do! In Elizabethan England, the Inns of Court were also the next stage in the education of the sons of gentlemen when they finished their time at one or other of the two Universities, Oxford or Cambridge.

Sir Frances Drake

The benchers or senior members of Middle Temple had been interested in the sea and exploration for a generation by the time Gosnold was admitted to the Inn in 1592. Twelve years before, Sir Frances Drake had returned from his voyage round the world. The hatch cover of the *Golden Hind* was presented to the Middle Temple to have pride of place as their 'cupboard' on which the book with the signatures of all those 'called to the bar' were recorded.

Middle Temple Hall, the setting for formal dinners

The Inns of Court were not just centres of legal activity, their members also enjoyed a good party. With so many young men from rich backgrounds living together, dinners in the Inn were lavish affairs with the Elizabethan delight in rich food and good wine much in evidence.

Elizabethan Food

Elizabethan cookery was generally sweeter than today's, meats were often cooked with fruits, producing a mix of sweet and savoury. New foods like tomatoes were considered doubtful, if not actually poisonous. Chocolate had not yet come in, except for medicinal purposes. The Swiss had not yet invented milk chocolate as we know it by adding milk and sugar to powdered cocoa beans and vanilla wasn't a period flavour either. Almond was the most common flavouring in sweets, used to make marchpane (marzipan) for sweetmeats. Spices from the East, cinnamon, cloves, and saunders (sandalwood) were use but these were all very expensive. Coffee and tea had come to England but were not yet used much except as medicines and even then they were very, very rare. Sugar was available, but was rather more expensive than honey, since it had to be imported. Grown as sugar cane in the Caribbean, it came to England as a 3 or 4 pound loaf. This huge sugar lump had to be grated into a powder before it could be used.

(by Micha K.)

Formal dinners in Middle Temple Hall at that time would consist of a series of courses, or 'removes', starting with potage or soup, and a first course of boiled or salted meat, chickens and bacon, pies, goose, pig, roast beef, roast beef and a sweet custard. The second course would be very similar, more roast lamb, capons and rabbits, chickens, peahens, baked venison in huge amounts and a sweet tart of fruit. Many of the meat dishes were served in a colourful and sweet jelly, made by following a 'receipt' or recipe like this one from a Tudor book.

To make Cleare Jellye

Take two calves feete and a shoulder of veale and set it upon the fyre in a fayre potte with a gallon of water and a gallon of claret wyne. Then lette it boyle til it be jellye and then take it up and strayne it and then putte thereto synamon, gynger and sugar and a little saffron to coloure it yellow after your dyscrecion. (from a Proper Newe Book of Cokerye, late 16th century)

All this would be helped down with many cups of wine and ale, and after the dinner, the entertainment would begin. On high days and holidays, such as the days after Christmas, these would take the form of revels, produced and performed often by the younger members of the Inn. In the winter, the players from the open theatres on the south bank of the Thames would be invited into the warmth of the Inns of Court or Blackfriars Hall nearby, for their performances. William Shakespeare's 'Twelfth Night' was first performed in Middle Temple Hall as just such an entertainment, and the poet John Donne was Master of the Revels at Lincoln's Inn at the same time as Bartholomew Gosnold was supposed to be busy studying law at the Middle Temple.

John Donne as a young man

Donne became a famous preacher later in his life but his late teens were spent living the good life in the London of Shakespeare, Marlowe and Johnson amongst the young gentry of the Inns of Court. In spite of all this revelry, the senior members or 'benchers' of the Inns continued to be very interested in the New World of the Americas. Ever since the Spanish had established colonies in Central and South America, and the French had started to explore the area now know as Canada, the English had been keen to plant a colony on the coast of North America. Another member of the Middle Temple, Sir Walter Raleigh had received from Queen Elizabeth the right to plant such a colony in the area which he named Virginia in honour of the Virgin Queen. Raleigh's first and second attempts failed and Drake picked up the survivors from Roanoke Island in what is now North Carolina, on his way back to England.

Raleigh did not give up and sent one further voyage to Roanoke Island. In 1587, English settlers including women and children were left there, although their leader, John White, came home to seek further supplies. Sadly, his attempt to take ships back to Roanoke were frustrated when Elizabeth ordered that no English ships could be spared for such ventures when Philip II of Spain and his great Armada threatened an invasion of England.

The English victory over the Spanish in 1588

In 1587, Drake attacked Cadiz and many ships that were preparing for the Armada were damaged or destroyed. The Spanish had planned to get to the Spanish Netherlands to pick up troops to invade Protestant England, ruled by Elizabeth I. When the Spanish Admiral died, Philip II of Spain chose the Duke of Medina Sidonia as the next High Admiral. He'd never been to sea and when he got on board he was seasick. In July 1588, the Spanish set sail but they hit an awful storm and many of the ships had to be repaired.

The fleet of one hundred and thirty ships, including twenty two fighting galleons, sailed in a crescent formation. There was little opposition as they approached Cornwall on July 29th 1588. Cornish fishermen saw the Armada and warned London by beacons along the coast because communications in the 16th century were very poor.

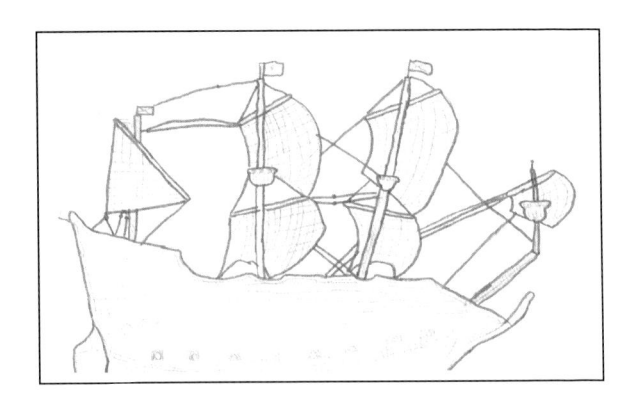

A huge Spanish fighting galleon from the Armada fleet by Tom R.

As the Armada went up the Channel, Drake attacked from Plymouth, but only two galleons were destroyed. The Spanish were low on ammo so they stopped at anchor off Calais to pick up supplies. The English siezed their chance and put anything that could burn onto old ships, sending them down-wind into the Spanish fleet. In panic, the Spanish had to cut their anchor cables to get away. Only one ship was actually lost, but the crescent shape crumbled and they were vulnerable.

Spanish ship on fire and sinking by Annabel B.

The Spanish could not escape west down the Channel but had to sail into the North Sea and round Scotland. Many ships were lost when they were driven onto the rocks on the Irish coast. Of the original one hundred and thirty ships, sixty seven never reached home in Spain.
(by Jack R.)

After the threat of the Armada had passed, John White did sail back to Roanoke, but it was too late. There was not much trace of the colony. But again the English did not give up their dream of establishing a colony in the New World. While Bartholomew Gosnold was studying at Cambridge and the Middle Temple, an Oxford geographer, Richard Hakluyt, was learning all he could about the exploration of the New World.

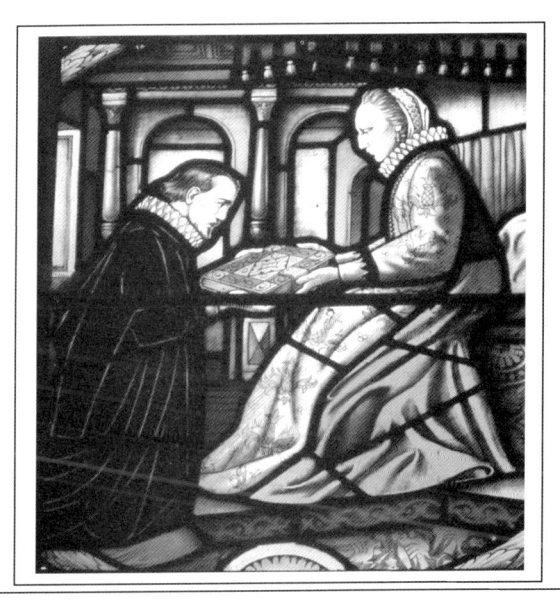

Richard Hakluyt presenting his book on Western Planting to Queen Elizabeth I, from the window in Willoughby Church, Lincolnshire.

Hakluyt was employed by Sir Thomas Stafford, Elizabeth's ambassador to France, as his Secretary and he used his time in Paris to collect all the French and Italian accounts of exploration he could find. To these he added the English accounts, and when he returned to England, he presented a copy of his *'Discourse of Western Planting'* to Queen Elizabeth

Hakluyt failed to influence the Queen, but he did not lose interest in exploration. When Sir Thomas' widow was given the Suffolk estate of Wetheringsett, near to Otley, she appointed a local lawyer, Anthony Gosnold, to help her sort out a problem with a troublesome rector. When the problem was solved with the death of the clergyman, she appointed Richard Hakluyt as Rector in his place and as a result, the leading expert on the accounts of exploration of America came to live near to Bartholomew Gosnold's home, with a close link to Gosnold's father, Anthony.

Just after Bartholomew left the Middle Temple, he met and married Mary Golding in her home county of Essex. She was the daughter of another East Anglian lawyer, Robert Golding, a member of the Inner Temple. His family already had strong links with the Gosnolds through the marriages of two of Bartholomew's great-aunts into the Essex branch of the Goldings. This branch was also well connected by marriage to the De Vere family, Earls of Oxford, providing Bartholomew with a network of family links of great potential value to a young and ambitious lawyer. Mary's grandfather, Sir Andrew Judd, was a wealthy merchant in London and founder of the Muscovy Company, trading with Russia. Bartholomew and Mary moved shortly after their marriage to Bury St Edmunds where her father owned property. It was in Bury that all but one of their children were born, their baptisms being recorded in the surviving registers of St James's Church, one of the two parish churches adjacent to the ruins of the Abbey of St Edmunds. The baptism of Martha was in April 1597. Sadly, this little girl died just before her second birthday. Her burial is recorded in April 1598. Robert was baptised in 1600, Susan in 1602, Bartholomew in 1603, Francisca (who died as an infant) in 1604, Paul in 1605 and the last, another Martha, in 1607. The one child whose baptism is not recorded was Mary, mentioned later in her grandmother's willl, who may have been born in 1596 or 1599 when the family was in Grundisburgh, a parish whose register has been lost.

Ironically, although we know the details of the Gosnold's family life through these records, we know less of what Bartholomew Gosnold was doing professionally in the years 1595 to 1601. It seems that he spent little time on the law, choosing to find a more exciting future by going to sea.

At that time, Ipswich and Harwich on the river Orwell and Woodbridge to the north on the river Deben, were busy ports with a growing trade with London and the countries of Northern Europe across the North Sea. The coastal trade in coal, grain and straw to fuel and feed the rapidly expanding capital city brought prosperity to these towns and a growing interest in exploration beyond the coasts of England and Europe.

In the 1580s, Thomas Cavendish, who was born near Ipswich, had sailed with the fleet that attempted to establish the Roanoke colony. He later sailed with another Ipswich merchant and mariner, Thomas Eldred, around the world, He returned to England in 1588, to be knighted by the Queen and celebrated as 'Cavendish the Navigator'. Exploration of the oceans had for many years been the monopoly of the West Country sailors, Drake and Raleigh,

Grenville and Gilbert, but by the end of the 16th Century, the ports of the Eastern Counties were taking the lead.

Thomas Cavendish, England's second circumnavigator of the Globe

      Bartholomew Gosnold must have gained 'sea-time' while he and his family were living in Bury, although the details are not well known. After the defeat of the Armada, Phillip II of Spain rebuilt his navy and the English mounted a major raid on the port of Cadiz, lead by the Elizabeth's favourite the Earl of Essex. Ten thousand men and one hundred and fifty ships attacked Cadiz to destroy Phillip's new fleet. The young Bartholomew Gosnold probably sailed with them as an ambitious young sailor keen to be involved in the venture. Although many of the Spanish ships escaped, Essex sank some and captured Cadiz and looted the city. In response, Phillip II then sent another fleet to attack England from their base in Lisbon but this was destroyed in an Atlantic storm.

At this time, England did not have a navy as we know it today. Elizabeth had decided to encourage English sea-captains to attack Spanish and Portuguese vessels returning with treasure from the Americas and the Spice Islands of the Far East.

Privateers and Buccaneers

At this time Spain was expanding her empire in the New World. This brought first a trickle and then a tide of gold and other goods back to Europe. This brought great wealth to Spain. England used her privateers, men like Hawkins, Drake and Raleigh, to attack and plunder Spanish ships crossing the Atlantic.

Much later when Britain acquired colonies in the Americas, they found that their policy of hiring and training privateers back-fired. Though many of the privateers were still getting paid, they plundered from both Spanish and English ships. Shipping was most at risk in the Caribbean, where the water was shallow compared to the Oceans, and the many islands allowed for quick inland raids on plantations. The privateers had become buccaneers but they were still really pirates. *(by Joe G.)*

Essex sailed again in 1597 to attack the Spanish fleet off the Atlantic islands of the Azores. The English missed the Spanish treasure fleet and returned home empty handed. But they also just missed the third Armada sent by Phillip to attack England's armies in Ireland. This too was scattered by an Atlantic gale forcing the Spanish to abandon their attempts to attack England and remove her Protestant queen. Bartholomew Gosnold was probably involved in all Essex's maritime adventures, and acquired a wealth of experience of seamanship, becoming an accomplished navigator and organiser of voyages.

He also became rich. By 1599, he had his own command, the *Diamond,* which he sailed as a privateer and took a rich Spanish prize. Her cargo was brought back to Falmouth and valued at £1,725, with Gosnold claiming his share of £200, a significant sum in Elizabethan England. Although he must have spent time at home with Mary in Bury St Edmunds, Gosnold's future was clear as a sea-captain rather than a Suffolk lawyer.

His uncle, Robert Gosnold had prospered in this role and built up a considerable estate of land around Otley, and added to his house, Otley Hall, grand enough now to entertain important visitors such as Sir Francis Bacon, the Member of Parliament for Ipswich and yet another lawyer from Gray's Inn. He was related to the Gosnolds through Bartholomew's mother who was a Bacon.

Bartholomew's father, Anthony, meanwhile seems to have been slipping into debt. There is a portrait of his uncle in old age – rich men can afford to commission portraits.

Robert Gosnold of Otley Hall, painted in 1610

Of Anthony Gosnold, or of his son, Bartholomew, there are no images from life, apart from this imaginative version by a 21st Century admirer!

Bartholomew Gosnold as a young man by Sophie P.

4. Seeking Norumbega

In 1599, Robert Gosnold was appointed Secretary to the Earl of Essex, Queen Elizabeth I's dazzling but unstable favourite. He resented the influence which the Cecils, William the old man and his son Robert, had with the Queen. Tall and good-looking, Essex mocked Robert Cecil's small size and hunched back. The animosity between the factions grew into open hostility. When Elizabeth realised that Essex had ambitions to rule her court, she deliberately picked a quarrel with him. When he turned his back on his Queen, she was furious and struck him across the face, telling him to 'go and be hanged'. Essex was so affronted by this assault, by a women even if she was his Queen, that he started to draw his sword, but was restrained.

Eventually Essex calmed down and was compelled to apologise. Elizabeth then sent him to lead her armies in Ireland with strict orders to pacify the Irish, which he failed to do. His failure sealed his fate and when he returned to London without permission, Elizabeth had him arrested and kept under house arrest in his London home.

Robert Gosnold was now the servant of a waning star and soon associated with a traitor. Essex led an armed attempt to take over the City of London, hoping that Sir Thomas Smythe, the Sherif of London, would support him with the City's trained bands of soldiers. Smythe refused and Essex was arrested, along with the Earl of Southampton, Shakespeare's patron. Southampton and Smythe survived, although they spent time in the Tower of London. Essex lost his head on Tyburn Green. Robert Cecil and his allies in the Court of an old and tired Queen had triumphed.

Sir Thomas Smythe, Sherif of London, whose mother was a step-sister of Mary Gosnold's mother

With the risk of attack by an Armada from Spain now very low, Cecil, Smythe and Hakluyt began to plan an attempt to establish an English colony in America. The age of rich men sponsoring such ventures was not quite over, and both Essex and Southampton were involved in the early stages, but with Essex dead and Southampton and Smythe in the Tower, other ways of financing such adventures had to be found.

Sir Thomas Smythe was immensly rich. He had lent Queen Elizabeth I a huge sum of money in 1588 to help finance the English ships which, together with the weather, defeated the Armada. He made his money in London, as a member of both the Skinners and the Haberdashers. These City Companies controlled much of the trade which passed through London and membership ensured business success. Smythe took an interest in every venture that was going, including the new idea of 'joint-stock companies'.

These were set up to raise the money needed for exploration and trade by selling shares to any who would buy them, rich individuals, City Companies, towns and even churches. These all invested, or 'ventured', their money hoping that, when the colony was established, successful trade would bring a rich reward to those who held shares. The first joint-stock company was the Muscovy Company, set up in the 1550s by Mary Gosnold's grandfather, Sir Andrew Judd, to finance the exploration of a way through to the Far East by going round the north of Russia, the North-East Passage. One of their ships did reach Archangel from where they set out for Moscow and reached the court of the Tzar of Russia, Ivan the Terrible. Trade between England and Russia developed and the Muscovy Company held the monopoly on that trade right through the Tudor and Stuart period.

Smythe invested in the Muscovy Company and became a Governor in 1600. When the East India Company was set up in London in the following year to develop and control England's rich trade with the Spice Islands of the Far East, Smythe became a governor of that too and Hakluyt was appointed Secretary.

Throughout the Elizabethan age, the English had failed to plant a colony in the New World. The Spanish and the Portuguese had gained huge wealth from their American Colonies and from pillaging the empires of the Aztecs and the Incas. The French had a foothold in the north, where Jacques Cartier had explored the St Lawrence River as early as 1534, but all the English attempts to establish permanent colonies had failed. There was one part of the North American coast which appeared on maps in Europe as 'Norumbega', just to the south of the area which the French had explored, in the region we now call New England.

Norumbega was said to be a 'city on a great river, populated by tall and clever people who traded in rich furs, spoke a language like Latin and worshipped the sun'. To the English it sounded just the place to do what the Spanish had done, establish a colony and acquire some riches for themselves. But did Norumbega actually exist or was it just a myth? There was only one way for the English to find out.

Cecil and Hakluyt began to raise the money from their wealthy contacts in London. Although Southampton and Smythe were still in the Tower, they too may have found ways to invest. Money is also said to have come from the Golding family through Martha Golding, Bartholomew's rich mother-in-law. With such strong family links, Bartholomew himself was the obvious choice to command the venture, although he had never sailed to the northern coasts of America.

Captain Edward Hayes had been there and had also written about the area. Hayes sailed with Gilbert to Newfoundland in 1583 and then turned south to the area where Norumbega was thought to be. His first account of the voyage was included by Richard Hakluyt in his *Principall Navigations*. In the 1590s, Hayes revived interest again by publishing a fuller account of the merits of the area in his *Treatise*, to promote the plan to '*plant Christian people and religion upon the Northwest countries of America*'. By 'Christian people and religion', Hayes really meant good English Protestants.

On the 26th March, 1602, Bartholomew Gosnold got ready to set sail from Falmouth in his ship 'Concord' which was leaky old vessel around thirteen paces long and six paces in width. It was crammed full of thirty tons of supplies for thirty two people including twenty would be settlers. It was definitely a tight squeeze. They sailed to what was to become New England in North America.   (by Frances M.)

Two other experienced Captains sailed with Gosnold, Bartholomew Gilbert and Gabriel Archer. Gilbert was Gosnold's deputy commander and had agreed that Gosnold and twelve of the gentlemen would be left in the New World to form a colony while Gilbert brought the *Concord* back to England. Gabriel Archer from Essex knew Gosnold and was also an experienced sea-captain. As well as his sailing skills, he would keep a record of the voyage.

Another gentlemen, John Brereton from Norwich, was on board to record the voyage and to serve as navigator. After studying at Cambridge, Brereton had joined the clergy, becoming Curate at Lawshall just south of Bury and not far from Hakluyt at Wetheringsett. Like Gosnold, he must have had some experience at sea to be useful as a navigator. Both his and Brereton's accounts provide a vivid record of the adventure, the birds and fish they saw and the people they met.

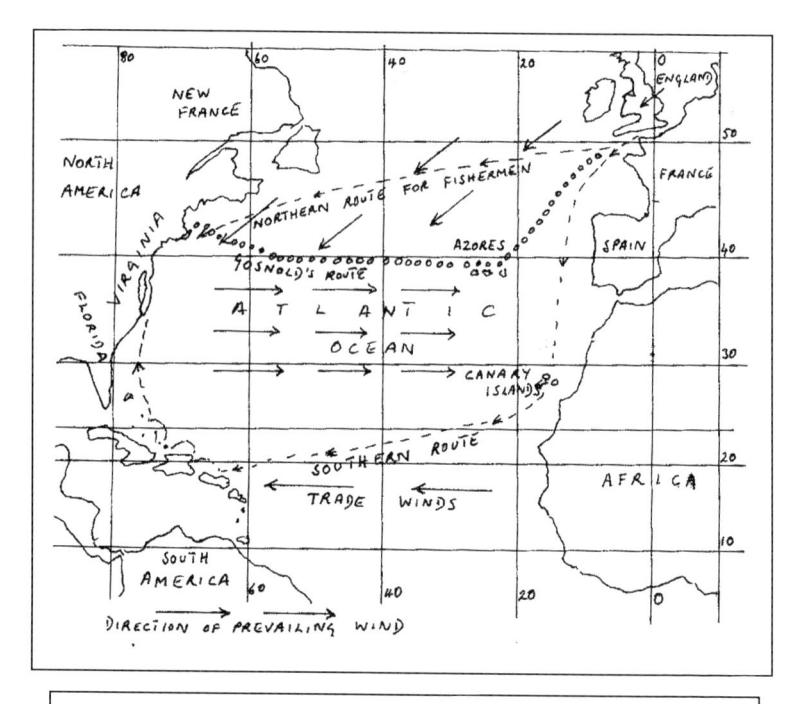

The two routes from Europe to America using the North Atlantic winds and Bartholomew Gosnold's new route via the Azores

From England, they sailed south west out into the Atlantic. *'The fourteenth of April following, we had sight of Saint Mary's, an island of the Azores.'* From there, Gosnold headed west across the Ocean. Most ships sailing to the Americas went much further south, to the Canaries and then caught the Trade Winds across to the Caribbean. But Hayes had advised Gosnold of the more northerly route which the fishermen took on their way to the rich fishing grounds off Newfoundland. There was a risk in Gosnold's choice. If he missed the north Atlantic easterlies, he would face headwinds driving him back towards the coast of Africa.

Gosnold still headed west and by early May, they saw the first signs that they were approaching land. *'We first saw many birds in bigness of cliff pigeons, and after diverse others as petrels, coots, hagbuts, penguins, mews, gannets, cormorants, gulls, with many else in our English tongue of no name. The eighth of the same the water changed to a yellowish green, where at seventy fathoms we had ground.'*

A few days later, they knew that they were close to the American shore, as they *'observed great beds of weeds, much wood, and divers things else floating by us, when as we had smelling of the shore, such as from the southern Cape and Andalusia, in Spain. The fourteenth, about six in the morning, we descried land...'* To their great surprise, they also made their first contact with native Americans.

'There came towards us a Biscay shallop with sail and oars, having eight persons in it, whom we supposed at first to be Christians distressed. But approaching us nearer, we perceived them to be savages. These coming within call, hailed us, and we answered. Then after signs of peace, and a long speech by one of them made, they came boldly aboard us, being all naked, saving about their shoulders certain loose deer skins, and near their wastes seal skins tied fast like to Irish dimmie trousers.'

The men in the 'shallop' or small boat, seemed friendly enough. *'They spoke divers Christian words, and seemed to understand much more than we, for want of language could comprehend. These people are in colour swart, their hair long, uptied with a knot in the part of behind the head. They paint their bodies which are strong and well proportioned.'*

After this promising first contact with people who clearly had already met European fishermen and somehow acquired their boat, clothing and a smattering of language, Gosnold sailed on west until on May 15th, they reached the mouth of a great open bay which seemed cut off from the open sea by a curving cape. *'Here, we took great store of codfish, for which we altered the name, and called it Cape Cod.'*

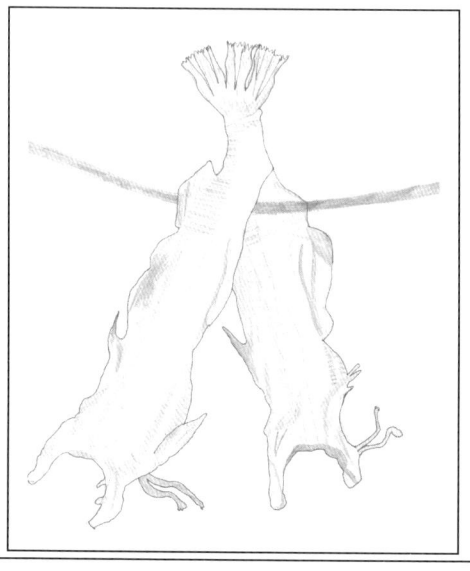

Cod, split and dried, to be packed in barrels for salting and taking to Southern Europe to provide fish on Fridays for Catholics

'We saw shoals of herring, mackerel, and other small fish, in great abundance. This is a low sandy shore, but without danger, also we came to anchor again in sixteen fathoms, fair by the land in the latitude of 42 degrees. This cape is well near a mile broad, and lies north-east by east. The captain went ashore and found the ground to be full of peas, strawberries, and whortleberries, as then unripe, the

sand also by the shore somewhat deep, the firewood there by us taken in was of cypress, birch, witch-hazel and beech. A young Indian came here to the captain, armed with his bow and arrows, and had certain plates of copper hanging at his ears; he showed a willingness to help us in our occasions.'

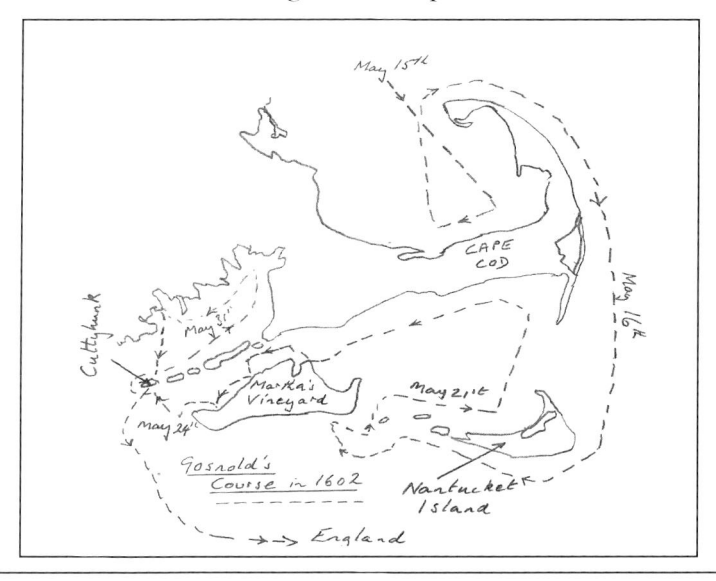

Map of the Cape Cod area showing the voyage of the Concord in May 1602, with the places named by the English, by Ben G.

Having sailed around the bay inside the Cape, Gosnold took the *Concord* out past the headland into the open sea and spent the next few days exploring the islands to the south of the Cape. The first, now known as Nantucket Island, seemed to be a 'woody place' without any particular features, to the west of which lay smaller islands which they named Tucker's Terror and Gilbert's Point after members of the crew. By May 21st, they had reached a larger uninhabited island.

'We named it Martha's Vineyard, a place most pleasant; we went ashore, and found it full of wood, vines, gooseberry bushes, whortleberries, raspberries, eglantines,

&c. Here we had cranes, ... shovellers, geese, and divers other birds which there at that time upon the cliffs being sandy with some rocky stones, did breed and had young. In this place we saw deer: here we rode in eight fathoms near the shore which we took great store of cod,...as before at Cape Cod, but much better.'

Was the island named in memory of the child that Bartholomew and Mary Gosnold had lost not many years before? Or was it named in honour of his mother-in-law who helped with the financing of the voyage? There is even a theory that it was named Martin's Vineyard, after John Martin, the master of Gosnold's ship. Whichever it was, Martha's Vineyard remained a remote island community for centuries which lived by whaling. Today it is a summer playground for the New England rich and there are now more commercial vineyards in Gosnold's native Suffolk than on this wind-swept island of stunning beaches and crashing surf.

To the northwest of Martha's Vineyard, they found a string of Islands, which they named the Elizabeth Islands after their Queen, and beyond a deep and sheltered anchorage they named Gosnold's Hope, now called Buzzard's Bay. The islands run from Naushon, nearest to the Cape, in a chain with Cuttyhunk at the western end, and it was here that Gosnold believed he had found the ideal site for his colony. Its island setting could be defended. There was water and a plentiful supply of fish. John Brereton's description of the island suggests a heaven on earth.

'We stood a while like men ravished at the beauty of and delicacy of this sweet soil, for besides diverse clear lakes of fresh water, meadows very large and full of green, grass, even the most woody places do grow so distinct and apart, one tree from another, upon green grassy ground...'

But was this Norumbega? Where was the *'city populated by tall and clever people who traded in rich furs, spoke a language like Latin and worshipped the sun?'* There was plenty of green grass, but no sign of gold, and the inhabitants of the islands were friendly, but not that impressive.

'There came unto us an Indian and two women, the one we supposed to be his wife, the other his daughter, both clean and straight-bodied, with countenance sweet and pleasant. To these the Indian gave heedful attendance for they showed them in much familiarity with our men, although they would not admit of any immodest touch.'

When the English shared their meal of salt cod flavoured with mustard with the Indians, they *'drank of our beer, but the mustard nipping them in their noses they could not endure: it was a sport to behold their faces made being bitten therewith.'*

There was also work to be done. *'The first of June, we employed ourselves in getting sassafras, and the building of our fort. The second, third, and fourth, we wrought hard to make ready our house for the provision to be had ashore to sustain us till our ship's return.'*

The fort and store house would shelter the twelve who planned to remain on the island with Gosnold through the winter until the following Spring. The 'sassafras' was the root bark of the sassafras tree which was of value in England as a medicine for treating syphilis and other diseases. Ironically, this is one of the few diseases that made their way back from the Americas to Europe. Most, like smallpox, measles, and influenza travelled westwards with Europeans to decimate the native populations of the Americas.

The remaining stores from the Concord were checked and divided up between supplies for those who planned to stay on the island and supplies for those who would sail home with Captain Gilbert. It soon became all too clear to some of them that there would not be enough for both Captain Gilbert's six week voyage home and enough to keep the colonists alive for the six months that it might take him to sail back again. So *'wrangling and ill-disposed persons,'* led a revolt against the plan to stay. They convinced the rest of them that all should head for England.

It was still only June but too late to plant a crop for that year's harvest. Bartholomew Gosnold must have tried to persuade them but they all wanted to get home. He was forced to abandon his plan to colonise the island. Cuttyhunk would not become another 'lost colony' because there never was a colony to lose. Although he must have been bitterly disappointed, Gosnold could at least complete the loading of the ship with sassafras and try to sell it profitably in England.

Sassafras was believed to have mysterious curative powers, perhaps because, on any one branch of the tree, three distinctive leaf shapes can be found; it has been used as a spice for 'gumbo dishes' and as the flavouring of root beer in the American Southern States.

'The eighteenth, we set sail and bore for England……the winds do range most commonly upon this coast in the summer time, westerly. In our homeward course we observed the foresaid floating weeds to continue till we came within two hundred leagues of Europe. The three-and-twentieth of July we came to anchor before Exmouth.'

There was further disappointment for Gosnold when they arrived in England and tried to sell their sassafras. Sir Walter Raleigh had been granted a monopoly on all saleable goods exported from 'Virginia', which covered the whole East Coast of North America from Florida to Canada. He therefore had a claim on this cargo and the right to impound it. This would prevent a sudden glut of sassafras knocking the bottom out of the market, or at least give him the right to charge an import duty. For a while, Raleigh claimed the cargo or what was left of it after the crew and passengers had removed what they considered to be their share, but eventually it was released and sold to provide Gosnold and his backers with some return on their investment and effort.

It was not enough to help his father who was still languishing as a debtor in the King's Bench Prison in Southwark. In purchasing the manors of Burgh, Clewes and Grundisburgh, he had incurred a large debt which he could not repay. One of the reasons why Bartholomew had gladly accepted the challenge of the Norumbega voyage may have been the chance to make enough money to get his father out of prison. When Bartholomew returned and had little to show by way of profit from the voyage, he wrote to his father to explain. His first letter was not apparently clear enough and he wrote again to explain some aspects of the voyage, the cold, the shortage of food and the harvest of sassafras. This second letter has survived – the only writing that we have from Gosnold's own pen.

7th September, 1602

My duty remembered, &c. Sir, I was in good hope ……as to have come unto you before this time; otherwise I would have written more… the country from whence we lately came…. In the mean time, you seem not to be satisfied by that which I have already written; first, as touching that place where we were most resident, it is the latitude of 41 degrees, and one third part; …yet it is more cold than those parts of Europe, which are situated under the same parallel: but one thing is worth the noting, that notwithstanding the place is not so much subject to cold as England is, yet did we find the spring to be later there, than it is with us here, by almost a month….It is as healthful a climate as any can be. The inhabitants there, as I wrote before, being of tall stature, comely proportion, strong, active, and some of good years,….are sufficient proof of the healthfulness of the place. First, for ourselves (thanks be to God) we had not a man sick two days together in all our voyage;…The sassafras which we brought we had upon the islands; … when we came to anchor before Portsmouth, we had not one cake of bread, nor any drink, but a little vinegar left.

And thus much I hope shall suffice till I can myself come…which though it be not so soon as I could have wished, yet I hope it shall be in convenient time.

In the mean time, craving your pardon,

I humbly take my leave.

Your dutiful son, Barth. Gosnold.

5. Planning the great voyage

Six months after Gosnold returned from Cape Cod, the last of the Tudors, Queen Elizabeth I, turned her face to the wall and died. She had ruled England for forty five years and remained the Virgin Queen, without husband or heir. Robert Cecil, her Secretary of State, had prepared for the moment of her passing by writing secretly to King James VI of Scotland.

A Short Profile of James VI

James Charles Stuart was born on June 19th 1566 at Edinburgh Castle in Scotland. His father, Lord Darnley, was murdered before he was one. His mother, Mary, became Queen of Scots. Her reign was short and James was made King on July 24th 1567, and crowned King James VI of Scotland, when he was only one year old.

James never knew his mother. Mary was imprisoned in England by her cousin Elizabeth I. She was executed for her part in the conspiracy to assassinate Elizabeth. Like many monarchs at that time, tutors raised James. He had four; the most influential was George Buchanan, a staunch Calvinist of sixty four with strict teaching methods. James grew up to be one of the most learned and intellectual men ever to be King. He could speak fluent Greek, Latin, French, English and Scots and knew some Spanish and Italian. He didn't need translators when conducting business with other heads of state. James started ruling Scotland when he was nineteen. Anne of Denmark became his queen and they had two sons, Henry and Charles.

(by Jack R.)

As soon as Elizabeth died, Cecil sent a messenger north to his new king. James VI of Scotland was now also

James I of England. James set out from Edinburgh to London to claim his throne, travelling with his court of Scottish nobles at a leisurely pace, stopping to be welcomed along the way by all who hoped to influence him by their generous hospitality.

James had no stomach for further war with Spain and stopped the system of privateering which had made English captains rich from their attacks on Spanish ships. He also decided to meet at Hampton Court with his Bishops and the increasingly demanding Puritans within the Church of England. When they could not agree, James announced that he would insist on the Puritans obeying the Bishops. He was sure that his authority as King would be undermined if the Bishops authory was challenged, and threatened to 'harry them out of the land' if the Puritans would not conform.

King James I of England

Peace with Spain meant that trade routes for the English could be developed without fear of attack by Spanish ships. Having changed Elizabeth's policy on privateering, James soon made it clear that her favourites were no longer to have any influence at court. He had Sir Walter Raleigh arrested and put in the Tower on a trumped up charge of treason. Those whom Elizabeth had imprisoned, including Sir Thomas Smythe and the Earl of Southampton, were released from the Tower.

James sent Smythe as his Ambassadour to Russia, a role which enabled Sir Thomas to make even more money. When he returned to London, he was granted the monopolies which Elizabeth had given Raleigh on all trade with the Americas. The way was open for planning to start on a new attempt to establish an English-speaking colony in the north of America.

But in 1605, Guy Fawkes and his fellow Catholic plotters came close to blowing up both King and Parliament. For a time, the life of the new nation of Great Britain, the united kingdoms of England and Scotland, was distracted by fears of a Catholic uprising. When the plot was discovered before the gunpowder could be lit, James and Parliament survived. The nation heaved a sigh of collective relief and the normal business of making money could resume.

A powerful group came together to promote the idea of creating a chartered company, with backing from the King, to establish new settlements on the American coast north of the Spanish in Florida and south of the French in Canada. Sir Thomas Smythe, Governor of the East India Company, brought his experience of setting up such a company, his fabulous wealth and all his connections with the City of London. Sir John Popham was Lord Chief

Justice of the King's Bench and backer of numerous ventures to the 'Norumbega' area. Sir Ferdinando Gorges was governor of the fort at Plymouth and had great influence in the West Country.

Exactly who did what is not clear, but Bartholomew Gosnold has long been credited with being 'one of the first movers' of the plan to set up colonies, and was well placed both by his links with Smythe and Hakluyt and his experience on the 1602 voyage to bring the key players together. It is he who is said to have brought in a young soldier of fortune, Captain John Smith of Lincolnshire, as a very experienced soldier and useful man to have on your side. Smith had little cash to invest but had a record of indestructability and practical leadership in tight corners which must have impressed Gosnold.

Captain John Smith's statue on Jamestown Island, Virginia

Gosnold seems to have approached his cousin, Edward Maria Wingfield, who knew Gorges and had fought with him against the Spanish in Flanders. Wingfield invested heavily in the venture and became a key leader. He was another lawyer from Lincoln's Inn, and typical of the self-important, well-connected gentleman whose family wielded influence in Suffolk and beyond. Gosnold, Wingfield, Smith and Hakluyt may well have met to plan their venture in Otley Hall.

The plan needed the support of the highest individuals in the land, men like Robert Cecil, now the Earl of Salisbury and James I's First Minister, and the Lord Chief Justice, Sir John Popham. Together they drafted a Royal Charter for two Virginia Companies, one based in London and one in Plymouth. The London Company had the backing of the City and was to establish a colony in the southern part of Virginia, somewhere in the river system which ran into the great bay of Chesapeake.

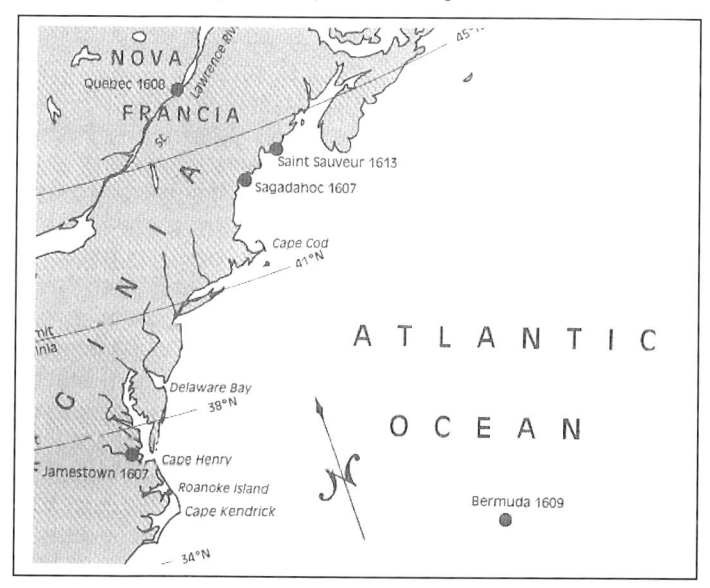

The regions allocated to the London Company, 34 degrees to 41 degrees North, and the Plymouth Company, 38 to 45 degrees north

The Plymouth Company was to establish a northern settlement at the same time, somewhere in the area which Gosnold and John Smith had explored and which Smith called New England. Each was allocated a strip of America between parallels of latitude and within fifty miles of the coast. Although the two regions overlapped, they together covered the whole of the American shore, not '*actuallie posessed by any Christian prince or people*'.

Over both companies, the Charter provided for a Royal Council of thirteen, appointed by the King, who would be based in London. Each was also to have its own Council of seven members nominated by the Royal Council from those who would go with the voyage to the new colony and govern its affairs when they got to the part of Virginia in which they were to settle.

The double-sided seal of the London Virginia Company

These seals decorated the Royal Charter which was granted by James I in 1606 to the Virginia Company of

London. It was a joint-stock company to establish a settlement or colony in America. The seal on your left reads: 'The noble royal seal of Britain, France and Ireland.' The picture is of James I. The seal on your right reads: 'On behalf of the deliberating body brought together by Virginia'. The picture is of the three lions of England, the lion rampant of Scotland and the harp of Ireland.

(by Tom R.)

    For the London Company, four names were included as 'patentees' in the charter. Two were soldiers who would play a part in the future of Virginia, Sir Thomas Gates and Sir George Somers. Rev Richard Hakluyt was included and Edward Maria Wingfield. Of the four, only Wingfield actually went to Virginia. Hakluyt initially decided he would go but changed his mind sending Rev Robert Hunt as Chaplain in his place.

The Virginia Company of London arms, from Willoughby Church

Once the charter had been signed, Sir Thomas Smythe could set about raising the money needed by selling shares. He was very successful, attracting investments from many of leading noblemen, clergy and rich individuals of the day. City Companies contributed, as did communities such as the Town of Ipswich, and many individuals. Captain John Smith invested £9.

With funds coming in, the leaders of the Company could acquire the necessary ships and stores and recruit the men. They chartered a solid, well-armed, merchant vessel of 120 tons, the *Susan Constant*, with a smaller merchantman of 40 tons, the *Godspeed*, and purchased an even smaller vessel, a pinnace of 20 tons, the *Discovery*, from the Muscovy Company.

Food and drink on board a 1600s ship

Each ship had to carry enough food and drink for passengers and crew for the whole voyage, carefully planned with individual portions.

Food: bread at 24 lb per man per month; meal at 30 lb per man per month; beef at 1 lb per man per day; pork at lb per man per day. There were peas and beans to go with the pork, three months supply of salted fish, oatmeal, wheat, 'olde hollande' cheese, butter, oil, vinegar, honey, sugar and rice. The crew were even allowed a couple of pounds of nutmeg, cloves and pepper to help disguise the taste the meat which would soon be rank on a long voyage.

Drink: beer at a pottle (half gallon jar) per man per day; cider at a quart per man per day; wine at a pint per man per day; no-one drank water if they could help it!

(by Micha K.)

Life on board

Life on board a ship like the Godspeed was not a pleasant experience. Ventilation could be a problem, especially during bad weather when the gunports had to be closed to prevent the ship from taking in water. If the bad weather lasted a while, the air could get very bad. It did not help that most got seasick in bad weather and vomit could soil the entire deck. Those who were not actually seasick were often made sick from the stench. Toilet facilities were often non-existent. The smell on the gun-deck was so bad that the crewmembers did not want to go there. The first mate usually purified the air with a red-hot iron that he dipped into a pail of tar. The smoke and steam from the bubbling tar helped to remove of the worst of the smell.

(by Alice V.)

The London Charter set out the terms for the '*colonie of sondrie of our people into that parte of America commonly called Virginia*'. James was impressed by their commitment to '*tende to the glorie of His Divine Majestie in propagating of Christian religion to suche people as yet live in darkenesse and miserable ignorance of the true knoweledge and worshippe of God and may in tyme bring the infidels and salvages*'. He also gave them authority '*to digg, mine and search for all manner of mines of goulde, silver and copper*' provided that they '*yeilding therefore yerelie to us, our heires and successors, the fifte parte onelie of all the same goulde and silver and the fifteenth parte of all the same copper*'. If America was to make the company rich, then James wanted his share.

The charter also approved their making their own coins and having exclusive trading rights with England.

The Virginia Quarter, minted in 2000 to begin the commemoration of America's 400th Anniversary showing the sailing of three ships.

Virginia Quay at Blackwall on the Thames, near to the point from which the Virginia Company's three ships departed in December

    Most important of all, the colonies should be able to defend themselves if attacked. There was still the threat that Spain would try to wipe out these small English settlements in what they still assumed was 'their' continent of America.

Finally, there was the important issue of who would lead the venture. Initially, it would have to be a sea-captain as getting them there was the priority. The Virginia Council could have chosen Batholomew Gosnold who had shown that it was possible to shorten the voyage by chosing the northern route. He had also sailed to the Azores and privateered in the Caribbean but there was another more experienced candidate.

Captain Christopher Newport, born in Harwich and based in Limehouse near London, was by far the most experienced sailor of his day. Although he had lost an arm in fighting the Spanish, he had brought more valuable prize ships back from the Caribbean than any other captain, and knew the route across from the Canaries and up to the Virginia Capes better than anyone. He had also been recently appointed as a Principal Master of the Navy. Looking for experience and competence, the Virginia Council appointed Newport as their 'Admiral' to lead the little fleet on the *Susan Constant* , with Gosnold as his 'Vice-Admiral' on the *Godspeed,* and Captain John Ratcliffe in command of the *Discovery*.

By December 1606, the fleet moored in Blackwall Reach, just east of London, was ready to sail. In the Captain's cabin of the *Godspeed*, Bartholomew Gosnold could have written a farewell letter to his uncle:

18th December 1606

My loving uncle, Sir.

As my father is so reduced in spirits, I will not trouble him with further burdens. Tomorrow, we sail on the tide for Virginia, to seek a fitting place for our habitation, to find the gold and pearls of which the poet wrote and to bring glory to our King. With me are two men who bear the name of

Gosnold, Anthony, my brother, and Anthony, my nephew and your grandson. Together, we trust to the goodness of Almighty God to preserve us on the voyage and in a strange land. I thank you for all your kindness in the past. Perhaps we shall meet again. In the meanwhile, I ask you to help my father in his distress and to look after Mary and our children.

I humbly take my leave. Your dutiful nephew,

Bartholomew Gosnold

6. Virginia bound

At first, they made good progress from Blackwall on the outgoing tide with the south-west wind behind them, going down the River Thames passing Gravesend and the fort at Tilbury. They sailed out into the North Sea and along the north shore of Kent to the North Forland before turning south into the mouth of the Channel. They did not get far before the headwind forced them near to the shore to shelter just off the shore in an area called the Downs. There they anchored to stop the ships being blown onto the treacherous Goodwin Sands.

The wind whipped up the waves into a choppy sea and the tiny ships rolled and pitched. They were all cold, wet and very sea-sick. Arguments flared up into open quarrels, especially between men like Smith and some of the gentry. Some, like the Rev Robert Hunt, not used to the sea, thought that they would die. He could have gone ashore as his parish church was not far away. But he chose to stay and his example helped to keep the peace and encourage the others. After more than a month of this torment, the wind changed to the east and Newport could lead them down the Channel and into the Atlantic Ocean. He was heading on the route he always took across to the Caribbean.

They sailed to the Canary Islands, as the old sailors put it 'go south until your butter melts, and then turn right' across the Ocean on the Trade Winds. By late March, they had reached the islands of the West Indies, with the argument involving Smith now blown up into an allegation of mutiny.

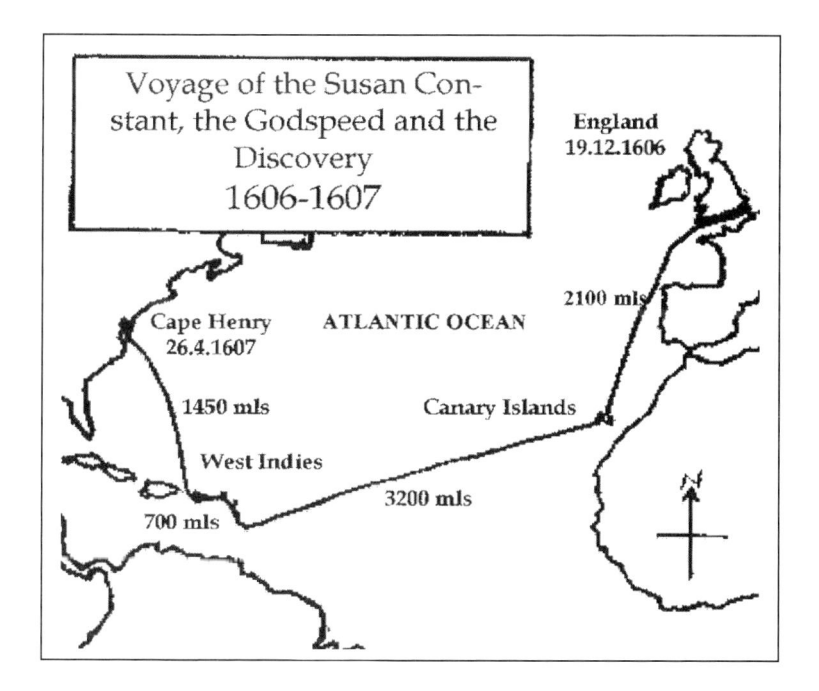

```
Voyage of the Susan Con-
stant, the Godspeed and the      England
         Discovery                19.12.1606
          1606-1607

                                    2100 mls
  Cape Henry      ATLANTIC OCEAN
  26.4.1607

         1450 mls       Canary Islands

      West Indies
                     3200 mls
       700 mls
```

Sailing north-west from island to island, they reached Nevis, where Newport tried to sort out the conflict involving Smith, without success. He could neither be 'persuaded to mount the gallows made for his excution', nor end his quarrel with Wingfield, so Newport had him kept in irons for the rest of the voyage.

For all this time, Bartholomew Gosnold sailed the *Godspeed* in Newport's wake, as did Ratcliffe on the *Discovery*. They reached the last of the West Indies Islands in early April and then set a course north crossing the Tropic of Cancer on their way to the Virginia Capes. Many of them had been this way before as ships returning to Europe from the Caribbean ran up the coast of America before catching the westerlies back across the ocean, but the coast was dangerous, known to many even now as the graveyard of the Atlantic. Between June and October, hurricanes rush in from the south-east and in the Fall, north-easterly storms hit the coast.

Storm off the Virginia Capes, the graveyard of the Atlantic

Even when the English arrived, in late April, a violent storm drove them north under bare poles until they were sure that they must have been carried past their destination. Ratcliffe and others of the gentry were all for giving up and sailing home, when, in the early light of dawn on the 26th April 1607, they *'descried the land of Virginia'*.

More by luck than good navigation, they had arrived off the mouth of Chesapeake Bay. They went ashore finding *'fair meadows and goodly tall trees with such fresh water running through the woods as I was almost ravished at the first sight thereof'* (George Percy).

They also met their first inhabitants of this area. When on their way back to their ships, they were attacked by *'savages, creeping up from the hills like bears, with their bows in their mouths'*. Gabriel Archer and one of the sailors were wounded but made it back to their ships.

Algonquian Indian warrior from John Smith's map of Virginia

For the next two weeks, the English used their open boat or shallop to explore the mouth of Chesapeake Bay. They erected a cross on the south headland which they named Cape Henry in honour of the Prince of Wales. The land was fertile and well-wooded, with a great number of different trees, flowers and fruits, plenty of fish and shell-fish, deer, turkeys, ducks and geese.

That evening, in the safety of their anchored ships, Newport, Gosnold and Ratcliffe brought out the sealed boxes, one for each ship, in which the Virginia Company's instructions had been carried out from England. Newport opened his box and read out the seven names of those nominated to the Council. Wingfield was an obvious choice as a member of the London Council and heavy investor in the venture. The three captains, Newport, Gosnold and Ratcliffe, were also predictable. John Martin and George Kendall as gentlemen were also included. But the surprise must have been great amongst them when Newport read out the name of the young man still held in irons on board the ship, John Smith.

They did not immediately release him. Six council members elected one of their number to be President of the Council for one year, Edward Maria Wingfield. He argued that Smith, having been a nuisance on the voyage out should be kept off the council and in chains. But Newport thought that they should follow the Company instructions and release Smith. He won them over. Perhaps he had known of Smith's nomination to the Council all along.

They also found the people who lived in the area both frightened by their coming and willing to welcome them with food and dancing. Exploring further up the wide river which ran into Chesapeake Bay, they searched for a suitable place in which to establish their settlement. Gosnold and Archer favoured a spot which had good soil, tall trees and wildlife of every sort. The only disadvantage was that the river was very shallow near to the shore so that the ships could not be anchored close in-shore. They called it Archer's Hope, but he and Gosnold were to be disappointed.

They found a low-lying, swampy island linked to the mainland by a neck of land. It had been used as a hunting ground by the native people but was unoccupied at the time of their arrival. Even better, the deep-water channel of the river ran very close to the bank so that they could use trees to moor the ships and unload easily. Newport and Wingfield favoured the place. Although it had no obvious spring of fresh water and much of the land was unusable swamp, as an island it would be much easier to defend both from the natives attacking from the landward side and any ships attacking from the river.

Mural showing the first communion service on Jamestown Island

The island was about fifty miles from the open sea and well-hidden behind a bend in the river. The first permanent English-speaking settlement in North America had found a home. They called it Jamestown, in honour of their king. Under an awning, Rev Richard Buck celebrated their first communion service following the words of Thomas Cranmer's Prayer Book. The Church of England had arrived in America.

Swamps and woods on Jamestown Island

Whitetailed deer on Jamestown Island

Newport took Smith and some men to explore the river in the shallop. While they were away, a group of Indians came onto the island and attacked their camp which had little more than a ring of brush-wood to defend it. Wingfield had taken the company instruction '*do not offend the naturals*' too literally and it was only when Gosnold on the *Godspeed* fired off one of the ship's cannons, that the Indians were frightened off.

When Newport returned, he organised the building of a fort which could be defended. Using the plentiful supply of timber from trees growing on the Island, the fort was built although the labour of felling trees and digging the trenches was exhausting for the settlers, particularly those who were not used to heavy physical work.

Jamestown Fort as it may have looked by Georgia R.

Jamestown Fort was built near the banks of the James River on Jamestown Island. It had a triangular wall made of tree trunks. They had to cut down the trees for the wall then they had to make a trench in which they put the ends of the trunks to make a palisade. Near the fort there was a church with a stone tower but all the houses were very simple so it would have been very hard to live there. Some people think that John Smith was the leader there at that time but historians have proved that he was not yet the leader, although he would certainly have helped with the building. The Spanish could have attacked the fort but they never actually did so. The Algonquian Indians did attack many times and the settlers used their guns to scare them off.

(by Oliver B.)

By June 22nd, with their settlement secure behind the walls of their fort, and their first crop of English corn set in the land they had cleared nearby, it was time for Christopher Newport to set sail for home. He had completed the task set by the Company, to take 105 men and boys to the Chesapeake and to ensure that they set up a defensible base there. One man had died on the way out from heat stroke having stupidly climbed a hill in the West Indies in the heat of summer wearing armour. But the rest had reached Virginia and seemed to be recovering well from the voyage. They had enough stores to last until Newport's return and prospects for the colony looked good. It was summertime on the Chesapeake.

Within three months, forty six of them would be dead. George Percy, the younger son of the Duke of Northumberland, kept a record of what happened.

6th August, John Asbie died of the bloody flux
9th August, George Flower died of the swelling
10th August, William Brewster wounded by savages and died, as did Jerome Alikock, an old man, also wounded; on the same day Edward Morris died suddenly
15th August Edward Browne and Stephen Galthorpe died

16th August Thomas Gower died
17th August Thomas Mounslie died
18th August Robert Pennington and John Martin died
19th August Drue Piggase died

The list of deaths went on. Some were gentlemen, others laborers and soldiers. At the rate that they were dying, none would be left by the time that Newport returned. Then, on the 22nd August, Jamestown lost one of the six remaining Council members, Captain Bartholomew Gosnold.

Bartholomew Gosnold was only thirty six when he died. He did not die from a disease called scurvy, but this probably weakened him, because of the lack of fresh food. He probably got sick with dysentery from drinking dirty water or he might have caught a disease from one of his men. Because he was a Captain, his men tried to keep him alive, but still he died! He was buried in Jamestown fort or just outside and all the soldiers fired off their guns around his grave as a mark of their respect for him.

(by Tom H.)

George Percy wrote of this terrible time: *'our men were destroyed with cruel diseases, as swellings, fluxes, burning fevers and by wars, and some departed suddenly, but for the most part they died of mere famine. There were never Englishmen left in a foreign country as we were in the new-discovered Virginia. Our food was but a small can of barley sod in water to feed five men a day; our drink cold water taken out of the river, at high tide very salty and at low tide full of slime and filth, which was the destruction of many of our men.'*

The fierce heat and very high humidity of a Chesapeake summer were quite new to the English.

Weakened as they were by months on a poor diet without fresh food, and without good clean water, they fell ill and died until there were fewer than five or six fit enough to defend the fort. At any point, the Virginian Indians could have attacked and captured or killed those still alive. In the end it was the same Virginian Indians who saved them. In Percy's words *'it pleased God to send those people which were our mortal enemies to relieve us with victuals, bread, corm fish and flesh in great plenty, otherwise we had all perished.'*

Wingfield was deposed as President and Ratcliffe took over. The death-rate dropped as the summer heat eased and the colony on Jamestown Island survived to wait for Newport to return.

Members of the eight Virginian Indian tribes who came to England in 2006, the descendants of the people who lived in the Chesapeake region when the English arrived in 1607.

7. Jamestown survives – just

In early winter, John Smith set out with two others on his first exploration of the country around the Chickahominy River which flowed into the River James. He was captured by the Indians and taken to their paramount chief, Powhatan. According to the account he wrote many years later, he was 'saved' from execution by the intervention of Pocahontas, Chief Powhatan's favourite daughter. Or was it a very different event in which Smith was 'executed' as an English Captain to be received again by the Indians as a member of their own people, as a chief himself incorporated into the social system of the Virginian Indians, or Powhatans, as they have come to be called after their chief.

However the incident is interpreted, it was the Indians who supplied the English with food and taught them how to grow 'Indian' corn when their own crops failed. It was the Indians' example that Smith followed when he dispersed the colony to survive on roots and shellfish when the corn ran out. It was the Indians' world that he explored in the shallop from Jamestown during 1608/9, as they rowed and sailed all over the rivers of the Chesapeake.

This pattern of near disaster followed by rescue at the last minute was to be repeated time and again in early Jamestown. When John Smith took over the leadership of the colony from John Ratcliffe in 1608, it was Smith's skill in negotiating with the Virginian Indians which persuaded them to supply the food the settlers needed.

Throughout this time, Smith had the company of Bartholomew's younger brother, 'Master Anthony Gosnold

– a most honest, worthy and industrious gentleman'. He survived the first summer's sickness and went with Smith on his journeys to meet with Powhatan. But in the winter of 1608/09, Anthony went across the river from Jamestown to Hog Island with nine others in a open boat. Heavily overloaded and caught in a violent wind, their boat sank. In the bitter cold about half a mile from the shore, they had little chance and all were drowned. Of the three Gosnolds who set off for Virginia in 1606, two were dead within two years of arriving.

Smith himself left Jamestown badly injured in 1609 and sailed back to England. Hundreds more English men and women arrived to join the settlement at Jamestown and they were clearly there to stay. The attitude of the Indians to the English hardened and no more food was supplied. If they acted together, the Indians could starve the English out. Through that terrible winter of 1609/10, Jamestown's 'starving time', the five hundred settlers tried to survive on rats and cats and snakes, and even human flesh, until only sixty were left barely alive. Help from England arrived just in time and once again, the colony was saved.

It was probably from the Indians that John Rolfe learnt to grow good tobacco using Spanish seed, the tobacco which provided the crop to turn the colony into an economic success. When Rolfe married the kidnapped Pocahontas the wedding brought a temporary peace with the Powhatan. This 'peace of Pocahontas' lasted nearly eight years. But when both Pocahontas and Powhatan were dead, the peace broke down and the Indians attacked the settlements of English in the massacre of 1622. That attack sealed the Indians' own fate as the English swept the 'murderous savages' out of their own land in the years that followed. The surviving settlers concentrated on growing tobacco and soon a booming export trade to England was providing Virginia with rich rewards.

Leaf tobacco curing in a tobacco barn

What happened to 'the other Gosnold', cousin to Bartholomew? He was still alive in Jamestown at the time of the marriage of John Rolfe and Pocahontas in 1614 as there is a reference in his Grandfather's will stating that 'his grandchild, Anthony Gosnold, was in Virginia' in 1615. After that, there is no further trace. He may have been among the 347 killed by the Indians in 1622 or he may have survived to raise a family in the Chesapeake.

Virginia became a prosperous, plantation economy, increasingly dependent on the labour of indentured servants, and then African slaves, to grow tobacco and cotton. It was in Virginia that the Continental Army of George Washington, with help from the French, defeated the British at Yorktown in 1781, and it was in Virginia that the armies of the Northern States accepted the surrender of the

Southern army at the end of the bloody battles of the American Civil War.

As Americans prepare to commemorate the 400th birthday of their nation, three strands come together: the one hundred and five English-speaking men and boys who set out from Blackwall in the winter of 1606/7, the Virginian Indians whose lands they occupied and whose lives they changed for ever and the Black Americans who first arrived in Virginia in 1619.

Each will tell their story. Each will use the commemorations for their own ends, the English Americans to celebrate 400 years of history, the Black Americans to remind the world of the realities of slavery, and the Virginian Indians to make clear that they are still here in this the land of their ancestors. But Jamestown would not have become a permanent English-speaking settlement without the planning of Bartholomew Gosnold, the skill as a sea-captain of Christopher Newport and the survival skills of John Smith.

8. Bones in the dirt

In 1699, the capital of the Virginia colony moved from Jamestown Island inland to Williamsburg. On Jamestown Island the trees and undergrowth gradually covered the ruins of the settlement. In the Civil War, the Confederacy built a gun emplacement on the site to protect their headquarters at Richmond further up the river from Union ships coming up the James River. The part of the island which included the site of the original settlement was bought by two sisters and left to the Association for the Preservation of Virginian Antiquities. Even in the 1980s, it was believed by almost everyone that the site of Jamestown had been washed into the river as the James eroded away the bank of the island.

Almost everyone, except the archaeologist, Dr William Kelso, who was sure that much of it must still be there. Around and under the earth mound of the Civil War fort, he started to dig in the dirt. Since the first dig in 1994, he has each year led a team of experts who have uncovered, and hence rediscovered, the original site of Jamestown.

Today, four hundred years after the English first came and set up their palisaded fort, a wonderful collection of over 700,000 artifacts, dug up from the dirt of the island shows what life was like for Gosnold and his fellow settlers from 1607 onwards. As Dr Kelso's team uncovered more and more of the site, they began to find burials which could be dated to the first years of the colony. One of these was clearly very special. In a shallow grave, a superbly preserved skeleton was lying within the outline of a coffin with the iron head of a Captain's staff at his side.

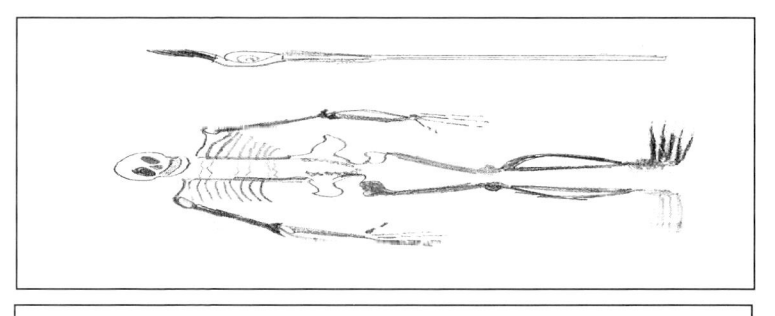

Could this be Bartholomew Gosnold's grave? (by Sam D.)

The experts identified the bones as those of a man of five foot three in his mid to late thirties. The Captain's leading staff matched similar early 17th century symbols of leadership. The setting was in the area where a number of burials had taken place. Was this the grave of Captain Bartholomew Gosnold, buried on 22nd August 1607, and honoured with a volley of musket fire to mark his passing?

There was only one way to find out and even that could not be certain. Today, DNA evidence is collected routinely from crime scenes and used to identify missing persons, but most nuclear DNA breaks down over time. The type of DNA called mitochondrial, which is found in bones, is more stable and can survive over a long time. It is also passed down through the maternal family line, from mother to son or daughter, but not father to son. So the hunt was on to find a sample of this sort of DNA from a known female relative of Bartholomew Gosnold.

The historical record showed that he had a sister, Elizabeth, who married Thomas Tilney of Shelley. From the research of historians, it was likely that this Elizabeth Tilney was buried in 1646 in the chancel of All Saints Church, Shelley.

The Parish Church of All Saints in the village of Shelley, Suffolk

There was one other Gosnold female relative, his niece, Katherine, who became Katherine Blackerby on marrying Thomas Blackerby, who was lord of the manor of Stowmarket. If her grave could be found in Stowmarket Parish Church it might yield a second DNA sample which could be compared with a sample from the Jamestown grave.

Permission was sought from the Diocese of St Edmundsbury and from the two Parish Councils to open of the graves of Elizabeth Tilney in Shelley and Katherine Blackerby in Stowmarket. Such permission is very seldom allowed and it was only because of the huge interest in the Gosnold story in both Suffolk and Virginia and the eductional value of the attempt to match DNA samples, that the authorities gave their permission.

Work in the Stowmarket Church proved disappointing. When the burial vaults were opened and examined by fibre-optic probes, they did not contain a coffin of a female of the right age, buried at the right time. Katherine Blackerby's bones could not be found. In Shelley Church, a coffin was found with a skeleton that was identified as a woman, although there was some doubt about the age at which she had died. Nevertheless, samples of bone yielding DNA were taken and the grave then very carefully refilled.

But when the DNA sample from the grave in Jamestown was compared with the sample from Shelley Church, there was no match in the DNA sequences. But was this the right body? No coffin plate or gravestone was found to identify the grave as that of Elizabeth Tilney. Samples of bone and close inspection of teeth showed that the woman whose remains were in the grave had probably died at about the age of forty. On that basis, she was far too young to be Bartholomew's sister who died aged about 70. But was this assessment of age accurate and were there any other sources of evidence?

The evidence seemed to suggest that the woman buried in Shelley chancel was not Gosnold's sister. Bone samples do yield other evidence, for example showing where in the country the individual grew up because what you eat leaves a trace of isotopes in your bones which is characteristic of the region. Comparison of bone samples from the two skeletons showed that both grew up in the same wheat-growing region, the Jamestown bones seemed to come from Eastern England. But we know that many of the Jamestown colonists came from this region, so there is so far strong circumstantial evidence but no convincing proof that the Jamestown grave is that of Bartholomew Gosnold.

The Jamestown excavations have produced a wealth of other details about the lives of the Jamestown settlers as they struggled to survive the first years of the colony. Thousands of items, some just fragments, some complete objects have so far been dug up or found in cellars and wells on Jamestown Island. They tell us about how the men lived, what they ate, how they built their houses and went about the business of establishing a settlement. They tell us how they died and were buried. They have come from the English and from the other Europeans who were at Jamestown and from the Virginian Indians who lived all around them.

Some are ordinary, pieces of pottery and scraps of animal bones from cooking fires. There are coins and trading tokens which provide dates and give an insight into the early business activity of Jamestown. There are glass beads and pieces of copper for trading with the Powhatan. Axe heads, chisels and files show how the work was done. The post-holes left by the first buildings show that they match the 'mud and stud' stuctures typical of John Smith's East Lincolnshire. This was a military base and that is reflected in the many weapons found, the firing locks of snaphaunce pistols, iron helmets and breastplates which the English wore and the arrow heads which the Powhatan fired at them.

Some of the items are medical, like the surgeon's instruments and some are very personal, like the silver fish-shaped item identified as an ear-picker for scraping teeth and cleaning ears which one of the richer settlers must have dropped.

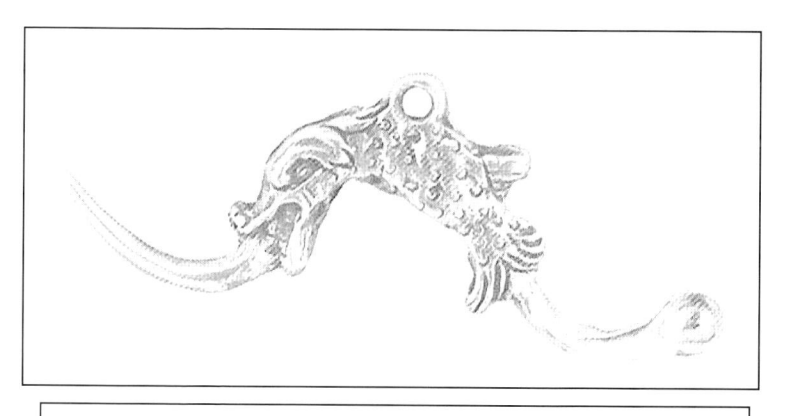

Replica of an ear-picker found on Jamestown Island

These extraordinary objects bring Jamestown to life again, as it was four hundred years ago and they provide astonishing detail. They are the legacy of over ten years of meticulous study by Dr Kelso and his team. He was right. Far from being washed away into the James River, America's birthplace is still there and ready to be the focus of the 2007 commemorations.

9. Living at the Hall

Otley Hall by Micha K.

Otley Hall, the home of the Gosnolds, is also still there. For more than five hundred years it has been a family house, not a museum, a hotel or an ancient monument in the care of the state. After Bartholomew's father died in 1609 and his uncle in 1615, the Gosnolds remained at the Hall for three more generations. During the English Civil War, they fought on the side of the King and were fined heavily by the victorious Parliament. Shortly afterwards, Otley Hall was sold by the Gosnold family and used by a succession of tenant farmers who largely left it as it was.

Otley Hall today

Otley Hall is set in 10 acres of gardens in the Suffolk countryside. The most impressive rooms are the Great Hall, the parlour and the forty foot galleried kitchen. Next to the fireplace in the great hall is where John Smith, Christopher

Newport and Bartholomew Gosnold are thought to have met to plan their journey to the New World.

The fireplace in the Great Hall around which the planning for the Virginia voyage is said to have taken place, by Jenny A.

There are many amazing features to the Hall including richly carved beams, linen fold panelling and 16th century wall paintings celebrating the marriage in 1559 of Robert Gosnold III and Ursula Naunton. There is even a mark on the woodwork to keep witches and other evils away!

The gardens are also stunning. There are croquet lawns, rose gardens and a moat walk. There are also many exquisite plants ranging from some lovely wild flowers to cultivated plants. The hall and the gardens have been looked after so they look as they would have done in the 15th century. Like most old English country houses Otley does have tales of ghosts. The ghost at Otley hall is called Abigail, she dates back 100 years when a woman was drowned in the moat. Her ghost was last spotted in 1975.

(by Alexander R.)

The Beaumont family moved into the Hall in 2004 with their two children Alexandra and Jasper. On three Open Days each year, the house and gardens are opened to the public and on other days throughout the year groups can book tours and functions. The Beaumont family not only lives from day to day in one of the finest Elizabethan houses in England, but also generously shares that house with many visitors, including those from Woodbridge School.

Living in Otley Hall is such an unusual experience that we asked Alexandra and Jasper how old they were when they moved to Suffolk. Alexandra: 'I was 8 and Jasper was 5. When our parents told us we were moving here, I thought it was untrue as I had always wanted to live in the country.'
Jasper: 'I thought that I would get lost – which I did, and was very excited.'
Alexandra: 'I thought at first it was very big and I think I may have seen a ghost. But it is not really a very creepy place to live in, although it can be scary, especially when unknown noises occur in the middle of the night.'
Jasper: 'I think it is really brilliant. There are lots of spiders and I get scared in bed because I thought that they would get in there, which they have been three times. At night, it's a good time to scare my sister!'
Alexandra: 'We can't mess up our rooms close to an Open Day, but Mum's restrictions aren't too bad! I don't really mind, I feel as if I am a part of history. We want to keep the fame and history of the house alive. The best thing is having space to run around in and feeling proud when people comment on the house. '
Jasper: 'It is fun to have lots of things to play with and lots of space, but I try not to boast about my house. The worst thing is people keep asking me questions about the Hall.'

Postscript

If you want to know more about what happened to the Jamestown Colony, read the four earlier books in this series *'Captain John Smith and the Founding of America'*, *'Admiral of New England – Captain John Smith and the American Dream'*, *'Mrs John Rolfe – better known as Pocahontas'* and *'Captain Christopher Newport of Limehouse, Virginia and the East Indies'*. All have been written and illustrated with the help of pupils from year 5 to year 8 in schools in Lincolnshire, Norfolk, Suffolk and Tower Hamlets, the parts of England from which the majority of the first Virginia settlers came.

Thirteen years after Jamestown was first established, the Pilgrim Fathers landed at Plymouth near Cape Cod and established their settlement. Ten years after that, the Massachusetts Bay Company settled the area to the north of Plymouth and founded the large colony which grew into the City of Boston, Massachusetts. Not long after Plymouth, the Catholics established their first settlements in Maryland. All these developments in early American history have their roots in the rich soil of Eastern England.

But the first permanent English-speaking settlement was at Jamestown in May 1607. The 400th anniversary of the founding of America will be commemorated in Virginia and in England in 2007, and the publication of this account of the life of Captain Bartholomew Gosnold is part of our conribution to those commemorations.

Bartholomew Gosnold - an outline chronology

1492	Columbus 'discovers' the New World
1509	Henry VIII becomes King of England
1547	Edward VI becomes King of England
1553	Mary becomes Queen of England
1558	Elizabeth I becomes Queen of England
1571?	Bartholomew Gosnold born in Suffolk
1580	John Smith of Willoughby born; Frances Drake completes his voyage around the world
1587	Raleigh's last attempt to establish a colony on Roanoke Island, but the colony fails; Gosnold enters Jesus College, Cambridge
1588	Defeat of the Spanish Armada
1590	Shakespeare's first plays, 1 and 2 Henry VI, performed; Gosnold entere New Inn
1592	Gosnold admitted to the Middle Temple
1595?	Pocahontas born; Gosnold marries Mary Golding and moves to live in Bury
1597	Martha Gosnold baptised, but dies just under two years later; Essex attacks the Azores
1599	Gosnold captain of the *Diamond;* captures Spanish ship as a 'prize'
1602	Gosnold sails on *Concord* to find 'Norumbega' and establish colony, but returns through lack of supplies
1603	James I, king of England
1604	Hampton Court Conference; peace with Spain; end of privateering
1605	Gunpowder Plot fails
1606	Gosnold recruited by Virginia Company as Vice-Admiral to take fleet to Virginia
1607	Arrives in Chesapeake in the *Godspeed;* Jamestown founded in May; Gosnold dies 22nd August 1607

Sources

We used the following sources to research this book

 Andrews K R *'Elizabethan Privateering'* CUP 1964
 Appelbaum R and Wood Sweet J, Eds. 'Envisioning an
  English Empire' Univ of Pennsylvania Press 2005
 Arber, Edward Ed.
  'Travels and Works of Captain John Smith ' 2nd Ed.
  A.G Bradley Edinburgh 1910
 Barbour, Philip
  'The Three Worlds of Captain John Smith'
  Houghton Miflin. 1964
 Doherty, Kieron
  'To Conquer is to Live' Twenty-first Century 2001
 Gookin, Warner F, *'Bartholomew Gosnold'* Archon
  Books 1963
 Horn, James *'A Land as God Made it – Jamestown and
  the birth of America'* Basic Books 2005
 Kelso, William and Beverley Straube
  'Jamestown Rediscovery 1994-2004' APVA 2004
 Kelso, William *'Jamestown – the buried truth'*
  University of Virginia Press 2006
 Price, David A
  'Love and Hate in Jamestown' Knopf. 2003
 Smith, Bradford
  'Captain John Smith' Lipincott. 1953
 Wright Hale, Edward
  'Jamestown Narratives'. Roundhouse. 1998
 Wilson, Harold C. *'Gosnold's Hope'*, Tudor Publishers
  2000

and the following websites:

Jamestown-Yorktown Foundation at
www.jamestown2007.org/ and at
www.historyisfun.org/jamestown/jamestown.cfm

'Historic Jamestowne' at
www.historicjamestowne.org/index/php

Association for the Preservation of Virginian Antiquities
at www.apva.org.

Virtual Jamestown Project at www.virtualjamestown.org/

The ARIES Project at
www.captainjohnsmith.co.uk

Thanks

Many individuals have helped us with this book and we would like to thank them all.

In Suffolk, UK

Mr Joe Chandler and Mr Nick Smith of Woodbridge School, Ian and Catherine Beaumont and Lucy Ruddock of Otley Hall, Sarah Friswell of St Edmundsbury Cathedral, Sheila Reed of the Suffolk Records Office, David Jones of Ipswich Museum

In Lincolnshire, UK

Mrs Molly Burkett and Mrs Jayne Thompson of Barny Books; Mr Geoff Allinson and his team at Allinson Print; Mrs Jenny Haden of Julian Bower for her proof reading and patience when American history got in the way of other priorities